AI and Big Data

Unraveling Insights Hidden in Massive Data Sets

Table of Contents

Chapter 1. Introduction

In an increasingly digital world, the intertwined fields of Artificial Intelligence (AI) and Big Data are presenting a tantalizing proposition - the ability to extract deep, transformative insights from staggering volumes of data. This Special Report is a deep-dive into this fascinating arena, demystifying the inherent complexities and highlighting the immense potential of this symbiotic relationship. Neither overtly technical nor excessively simplistic, it navigates the perfect balance, to provide you with an accessible, insightful, and practical guide to understanding and leveraging AI and Big Data. From unlocking hidden patterns in mammoth data sets to predicting future trends, this report is your all-encompassing guide to the world of AI and Big Data - a 'must-add' to your digital library, that will empower you to harness the power of data like never before.

Chapter 2. Unveiling the Concepts: AI and Big Data Simplified

AI and Big Data are two powerful technologies that, in concert, offer unimaginable opportunities to businesses, individuals, and societies. Understanding these concepts essentially forms the first step towards leveraging them in a beneficial manner.

2.1. Understanding Artificial Intelligence

Artificial Intelligence (AI) is an expansive field of computer science that replicates human intelligence processes in machines. In other words, AI involves programming computers and other machines to "think" like humans and simulate human behavior. The main objectives of AI include learning, reasoning, problem-solving, perception, and language understanding.

AI is typically categorized into two primary types:

- Narrow AI: These are systems designed to carry out simple tasks such as voice recognition. The most familiar forms of Narrow AI are Siri and Alexa.

- General AI: These are systems or devices which can handle any intellectual task that humans can do. They are able to understand, learn, adapt, and implement knowledge.

AI operates on the concept of machine learning, which involves teaching a machine how to learn and make decisions independently. Deep learning, a subset of machine learning, utilizes artificial neural network architectures to carry out the process of machine learning.

2.2. Understanding Big Data

'Big Data' refers to incredibly large data sets that are too complex to be handled by traditional data-processing software. These data sets are characterized by the three Vs - Volume, Velocity, and Variety.

- Volume: This refers to the quantity, or vast amounts of the data generated every second.

- Velocity: This concerns the speed with which data is generated and must be processed to meet demand.

- Variety: This pertains to the different types of data (structured, semi-structured, and unstructured) that are generated.

With Big Data, analysts, researchers, and businesses are able to identify patterns, trends, and associations, particularly relating to human behavior and interactions.

The relationship between human behavior and digital processes creates a large quantity of data on a daily basis. By employing AI algorithms and tools, businesses can turn this mountain of data into actionable insights.

2.3. Interaction of AI and Big Data

The interplay of AI and Big Data unlocks unprecedented benefits. AI applies intelligence to Big Data to sift through the noise and find meaningful insights, while Big Data provides the necessary raw material for AI to learn, adapt, and evolve.

AI, fueled by machine learning algorithms, uses the large volumes of data to learn patterns, generate insights, and make predictions. Therefore, Big Data acts as the feeding ground for AI, and in return, AI provides analytical capabilities to discover valuable insights within Big Data.

2.4. Potential Applications of AI and Big Data

AI enhanced with Big Data can be utilized in a wide range of applications:

- Healthcare: Predictive analytics can help in foreseeing outbreaks of epidemics, develop new drugs, and offer personalized medicine.

- Finance: Identifying patterns in market trends or fraud detection is made faster and more accurate.

- Agriculture: AI can analyze soil samples, weather forecasts, and predict crop growth patterns.

- Retail: Customer behavior can be analyzed to offer personalized recommendations and improve customer service.

Understanding the fundamental concepts of AI and Big Data is the first step towards leveraging these technologies. With this grasp, numerous sectors can harness this digital revolution to open plethora of opportunities obscured by the volumes of data.

2.5. Conclusion: The Future with AI and Big Data

In a world that is becoming increasingly centered on technology, the intertwined arenas of AI and Big Data become less of a trend and more of a necessity. But as we tread the path of digital transformation, it is crucial to acknowledge the challenges that these technologies pose and address them cohesively.

AI is playing a significant role in processing, analyzing, and making sense of Big Data. On the flip side, Big Data is providing AI the essential fodder it needs to learn and grow.

While it may seem overwhelming, this combination of technologies presents both individuals and organizations with unprecedented opportunities for growth and innovation. Through further research and development, the potential of AI and Big Data will continue to unfold, and our understanding will continue to evolve.

In conclusion, AI and Big Data, when leveraged appropriately, can bring about transformative changes spanning various sectors, making it paramount to understand these complex technologies. As we progressively untangle these intricacies, each of us will be better positioned to harness the power of AI and Big Data to enrich our lives and businesses.

Chapter 3. The Interface of AI and Big Data: An Intersection of Power

AI and Big Data are an inexorable team, two complementary forces that together can alter the face of your business landscape. As we delve into their dynamic, we start to realize the profound implications of their combined strength - and the reason why they're at the helm of today's technological revolution.

3.1. Understanding the Basics

For the uninitiated, Artificial Intelligence (AI) can conjure images of fictional, sentient robots, driven by a consciousness perfectly mimicking - or superseding - human intelligence. In reality, AI is an umbrella term for numerous technologies that make machines smart. Who teaches them this 'smartness'? Big Data. Big Data refers to massive amounts of data that typical data processing tools cannot handle. With soaring Internet usage and the proliferation of IoT-enabled devices, we are producing a staggering 2.5 Exabytes (approximately 2.5 billion Gigabytes) of data per day, a gold mine of potential insights waiting to be uncovered.

3.2. The Synergy of AI and Big Data

AI and Big Data are akin to a teacher-student dynamic. With Machine Learning (ML), a subset of AI, computers are tutored how to learn patterns and make predictions by parsing through Big Data without explicit programming. This dynamic interplay, bestowing ML algorithms the power to learn and unlock meaningful insights through training on large datasets, serves as the cornerstone of some pretty remarkable developments across industries, from personalized product recommendations in e-commerce to predictive maintenance in manufacturing.

3.3. Impact on Businesses

The blend of AI and Big Data is redefining the way businesses operate and compete in the market. It's empowering companies, large and small, to become information-driven, to make well-informed decisions and unprecedented predictions. A quick look at the retail industry will show how e-commerce giants are leveraging AI to capture customer preferences, predict trends, and provide recommendations - all sourced from analyzing significant volumes of customer data.

Even industries, such as healthcare, which once remained relatively untouched by such advancements, are now spurred towards an era of personalized medicine, predicting disease outbreaks, and optimizing healthcare delivery. AI-powered predictive analytics can detect patterns in historical and real-time data, helping physicians to diagnose diseases accurately, identify high-risk patient groups, and devise effective treatment plans.

3.4. The Intersection: Where Power is Amplified

The convergence of AI and Big Data is crafting a new order of machine intelligence and creating unimaginable opportunities. Compliance with strict data regulatory standards, efficient and secure data storage, sophisticated AI algorithms - all come together to build an intricate mesh at this intersection, eventually shaping the way we deal with big data.

One such impactful convergence is observed in predictive maintenance, where AI's ability to extract actionable insights from huge data sets has opened up a new avenue for industries heavily reliant on machinery. The algorithm learns the normal behavior of machine components and predicts deviations, potentially avoiding unscheduled downtime and extending the life of the equipment.

3.5. Challenges at the Intersection

Yet, the path is not bereft of obstacles. Data privacy and security are significant issues that technologists grapple with. The coupling of AI with Big Data creates clusters of data - an attractive target for cybercriminals. Additionally, the current pace of evolution brings forward critical ethical dilemmas and legal complications. Automation, fueled by AI, suggests a future with fewer human jobs. Adhering strictly to globally-accepted AI ethics and privacy guidelines, and establishing a balanced AI-human workforce, seems to be the pragmatic way ahead.

3.6. Conclusion

No one could have predicted the explosive growth of AI and Big Data. The two, acting in synergy, are redefining the art of the possible, from healthcare to finance, offering breakthrough insights, making businesses smarter, lives better. While hurdles are there at the intersection of AI and Big Data, the potential of this convergence is not to be understated.

As we stand on the precipice of this new and exciting frontier, it is important to remember: emerging technologies might open doors to uncharted territories, but they must always be used ethically and responsibly, ensuring a better tomorrow for all.

Chapter 4. Ingenious Algorithms: The Mechanics of AI

Artificial Intelligence (AI) is adjudicated on the foundation of ingenious algorithms, which power its underlying mechanics - from data processing and pattern recognition to decision making and learning capabilities. These algorithms represent not just the 'brains', but the 'nerves' and 'muscles' of AI systems, as they guide data flow, extract insights and propel actions.

Chapter 5. The Building Blocks of AI Algorithms

A fundamental understanding of AI algorithms commences with an efficient tale of its building blocks. These include Data, Features, Models, and Evaluation metrics.

5.1. Data

In AI, data is king. Colossal amounts of it power present-day AI systems. From user clicks on a website to patient symptoms in a hospital, data is all around us. AI algorithms use this data as the basis for learning about the world, building models, and making decisions.

5.2. Features

The next step in the data processing journey involves feature extraction. Essentially, features are variables or characteristics that are extracted from raw data and used to represent patterns or relationships. The quality and relevance of features have a profound influence on the learning and decision-making ability of AI algorithms.

5.3. Models

Models create the core structure of AI systems. They are mathematical constructs or computational frameworks which are trained on the extracted features to generate predictions, classify data or even mimic human-like decision making.

5.4. Evaluation metrics

How can we quantify the success or failure of an algorithm? This is where evaluation metrics come into play. They score the output of AI models based on prescribed criteria, establishing the strength or weakness of the model performance.

Chapter 6. Basic Algorithms in AI

Algorithms power the central mechanics of AI. Key among these are Supervised Learning, Unsupervised Learning, Reinforcement Learning, and Deep Learning.

6.1. Supervised Learning

Imagine an algorithm that is supervised or guided along its learning path, much like a student under a teacher. That's Supervised Learning. This algorithm uses labeled data, where both the data and the outcome are known, to learn the mapping function between inputs and outputs.

6.2. Unsupervised Learning

Here, the algorithm is on its own, without any labeled data to guide it. Instead, it identifies patterns and relationships in the input data itself, grouping similar data points together - a process known as clustering.

6.3. Reinforcement Learning

An adventurous learner, the Reinforcement Learning algorithm goes through a trial-and-error learning process. The algorithm is rewarded or penalized (reinforced) based on its decisions, encouraging it to learn the best policy or course of action over a series of decisions.

6.4. Deep Learning

Deep Learning is inspired by the human brain. It uses layers of artificial neural networks to understand and make sense of complex, raw data. It's the algorithm responsible for monumental feats like recognizing images, understanding human speech, and enabling self-driving cars.

Chapter 7. Advanced Algorithms and Techniques

With the foundational understanding in place, let's elevate our viewpoint to comprehend advanced techniques such as Support Vector Machines, Decision Trees, Random Forests, Gradient Boosting, and Ensemble Methods.

7.1. Support Vector Machines

A Support Vector Machine (SVM) is like a line or a boundary that best separates data into distinct classes. In a multi-dimensional data space, an SVM constructs hyperplanes to achieve the best separation, providing a robust way to classify data.

7.2. Decision Trees and Random Forests

A Decision Tree works on the concept of branching decisions, much like a game of 20 questions. The tree starts at a single point (root) before branching out based on features of the data, leading to a decision. Random Forests take this concept further by creating an 'ensemble' of decision trees, and then aggregating their outputs.

7.3. Gradient Boosting and Ensemble Methods

Gradient Boosting is a method that improves the model's performance by sequentially correcting its predecessor's errors, much like a relay race in athletics. Ensemble methods, on the other hand, combine the predictive power of multiple weak models into a single, stronger one.

Chapter 8. Conclusion

The echelons of AI fortress are diverse, each employing different techniques for disparate tasks. However, they all have one underlying feature – the intelligent arithmetic of algorithms. These ingenious algorithms operate with mechanical precision, turning the cogs of data into actionable insights, building models for decision making, and continuously adapting in their quenchless thirst for knowledge. Having decoded the mechanics of AI, the next chapter will introduce you to Big Data, the gigantic goldmine of boundless information waiting to be explored.

Chapter 9. The Art of Amassing: How Data Goes 'Big'

In the digital age, if knowledge is power, then data is definitely the currency. Data is everything and everywhere; it surrounds us, like the air we breathe. Before delving deeper into the matter, it is crucial to note that what we commonly refer to as Big Data isn't just about 'large' quantities of data, but also about the complexity, diversity, and speed at which it is generated.

9.1. From Megabytes to Zettabytes

Traditionally, data has been relatively small and manageable, residing comfortably in databases and excel files. It proliferated from very confined and recognizable sources: documents, archives, records. This small structured universe of data fit snugly into gigabytes and terabytes. However, the paradigm swiftly shifted as the prevalence of Internet-connected devices, social media outlets, and digital platforms grew in number, producing constant streams of structured, semi-structured, and unstructured data - thus propelling us towards the zettabyte era.

The data generated from our online footprint - be it from online shopping, social media interactions, online searches, or even simply through the digital trails we leave just by being connected - aggregates to an analogy of data amassed in an unimaginably enormous scale. Adding to this avalanche, the data not only inflates from traditional computing devices but also from a vast array of sensors and Internet of Things (IoT) devices, which contribute significantly to the volume, variety, velocity, and veracity of data generated daily.

In essence, we can think of Big Data as this totality of data, existing in diverse formats, growing exponentially - a vast ocean of information promising valuable insights - the proverbial needle of wisdom often hidden in a haystack of noise.

9.2. The Diversity of Data

Data is as diverse as the activity generating it. Data can be structured, semi-structured, or unstructured. Structured data refers to data that is rigidly formatted and can be readily and easily absorbed into database systems (numbers, dates, strings of words, and so on). Traditional databases and spreadsheets pivot around structured data.

However, not all data conforms to this neat organization. Semi-structured data like JSON or XML have some level of organization but not as explicit or strict as structured data. Emails, blog posts, tweets - digital pieces of information with some inherent structural elements but not entirely conforming to the traditional format of structured data, fall into this category.

The rise of digital media has led to the explosion of unstructured data - be it text, images, video, or audio. This data lacks a pre-defined model or is not organized in a pre-defined manner. Social media feeds, video content, customer reviews, web pages - they all contribute to the chunk of unstructured data.

9.3. The Power of Many: Networked Data

The value of data often increases when it is connected with other data - a phenomenon also known as networked data. For instance, a single tweet or a single point in a massive dataset might not yield much information. But network that tweet to the user's profile, their followers, their geographical location, and suddenly you start to see patterns and potential insights. In the same vein, networked sensor data from IoT devices can give a comprehensive view of environmental factors. Relationships, when drawn between diverse datasets, often unveil remarkable insights.

9.4. Tools and Infrastructure: Taming the Beast

As the domain of Big Data expanded to include larger, more complex, and more diverse sets of data, traditional data management tools proved woefully inadequate. The situation led to the evolution of new tools and technologies specifically designed to handle Big Data.

These include:

1. Frameworks like Hadoop - which can process large volumes of data in a distributed computing environment.

2. Databases such as NoSQL, which can handle unstructured data more efficiently.

3. Advanced algorithms, machine learning tools, and AI for extracting insights from massively large and diverse datasets.

4. Data visualization tools, which can generate interactive dashboards and visual reports based on Big Data analysis.

9.5. Legal and Ethical Considerations

The collection, storage, and use of massive amounts of data bring up important ethical and legal considerations. As we navigate the Big Data terrain, we need to address issues such as privacy, data protection, informed consent, data de-identification, and equitable access to Big Data's benefits.

9.6. Big Data: The Revolution is Just Beginning

To conclude, we find ourselves in an age where the data keeps getting 'Bigger'. The road to amassing Big Data is laden with various challenges, yet it's a road we traverse willingly for the promise of transformative insights, novel solutions, and a peek into future trends. How well we harness the potential of Big Data and how responsibly we navigate its inherent challenges will determine the impact of this exciting digital revolution.

Chapter 10. A Deep Dive into Data Mining Techniques

Before steering into a discussion about various data mining techniques, it is crucial to understand what it exactly entails. Data mining is the process of sifting through raw data to uncover appropriate and meaningful information. By using an array of complex algorithms, businesses can analyze hidden patterns in large datasets that conventional analytics might miss out on. These distilled, value-driven insights then prove instrumental in making strategic business decisions.

10.1. Understanding the Importance of Data Mining Techniques

Data mining holds significance in today's data-driven world due to numerous reasons:

- Reveal Hidden Patterns: One of the primary reasons companies mine data is to discover hidden patterns that are not ordinarily apparent. These patterns can provide new insights into business operations and aid in identifying potential opportunities or challenges.

- Enhance Decision Making: By analyzing vast volumes of data and deciphering meaning from it, companies can make more informed decisions, often leading to enhanced profitability.

- Predict Future Trends: Effective data mining can reveal patterns that indicate future trends, helping businesses prepare for emerging opportunities or potential disruptions.

10.2. Classification of Data Mining Techniques

Data mining techniques can be primarily classified into two categories: predictive and descriptive.

- Predictive Analysis: This technique makes predictions about future outcomes based on historical data. Techniques employed for predictive analysis may include regression, time-series data mining, and machine learning algorithms.

- Descriptive Analysis: This data mining technique focuses on identifying patterns and relationships in the present dataset. It aims to provide insights into the data that can lead to proper understanding and interpretation. Examples can include clustering, anomaly detection, association rule mining and sequential pattern mining.

10.3. The Most Popular Data Mining Techniques

With a basic understanding of what data mining involves and the classification of various techniques, we now move on to discussing some of the most popular and widely used data mining techniques:

1. Regression Analysis: Regression analysis is a predictive modelling technique that attempts to find a relationship between a dependent (target) and an independent variable (predictor). It is traditionally used in statistics but also finds use in machine learning under supervised learning algorithms.

2. Anomaly Detection: Anomaly detection is a technique of identifying unusual patterns that do not conform to standard patterns. These anomalies, or outliers, can be indicative of significant incidents, including bank fraud, medical problems, or

errors in a text

3. Clustering: Clustering is a significant technique in the world of data mining. It is a method used to divide the data into sets, or "clusters", wherein the data with similar characteristics are together and those with different traits are in other clusters.

4. Association Rule Mining: Association rule mining is a technique to uncover how items are associated with each other. It works by identifying the frequent if-then associations, which are called association rules. It is a popular method in market basket analysis, where it is used to analyze customer shopping patterns.

5. Decision Trees: A decision tree is a flowchart-like tree structure wherein each internal node denotes a test on an attribute, each branch represents an outcome of a test, and each leaf node holds a class label. Analysis of more massive data becomes manageable using decision trees.

10.4. Data Mining Software and Tools

There exist numerous data mining tools that help businesses extract valuable information from voluminous data. Some of the renowned ones include RapidMiner, Knime, Orange, WEKA, and SAS Data Mining.

10.5. Conclusion

Data Mining is an integral part of Big Data, aimed at offering a better understanding of the large datasets and generating added value from them. With the right tools and understanding of these techniques, businesses can augment their decision-making ability, better understand their customers, and optimize their resources to achieve more significant growth.

It is critical to remember, however, that the results derived from data mining are as effective as the quality of data fed into the process. Hence, it is equally essential to focus on improving data quality and ensuring accurate data collection procedures are in place. As data continues to grow exponentially, so will the utility and importance of data mining techniques and tools.

Chapter 11. The Power of Prediction: AI and Forecasting

The convergence of AI and Big Data has given rise to powerful predictive capabilities, reshaping business strategies, policy-making, and day-to-day decision making. However, to fully harness these predictive capabilities, one must navigate through the multifaceted disciplines of machine learning, data analysis, and statistical forecasting.

11.1. Understanding AI-Powered Predictions

AI-powered predictions are built on the foundation of machine learning, a subset of AI that involves the process of teaching a machine to discern patterns by feeding it vast volumes of data. Machine learning models, such as regression, neural networks and decision trees, are used to project specific outcomes based on historical data. These models observe recurrent patterns in the data and, over time, learn to associate these patterns with particular outcomes.

The performance of these predictive models rests on the quality and quantity of data they analyze – the richer the data, the more accurate the projections. Therefore, the rise of Big Data, characterized by increasingly accessible datasets of immense size and diversity, is driving advancements in prediction accuracy.

11.2. Machine Learning and Predictive Modelling

Machine learning is the keystone of predictive modeling. While conventional programming feeds computers explicit instructions to execute in deterministic ways, machine learning employs inductive reasoning where insightful conclusions are drawn from vast datasets.

For example, a traditional weather forecasting program might be encoded with set rules, such as "If barometric pressure drops and humidity rises, predict rain." However, machine learning takes a hugely complex, multidimensional dataset, comprising historical and current weather data globally and outputs a prediction based on learned patterns.

The relationship between predictors (independent variables) and outcomes (dependent variables) are captured in a model. Training a model involves providing it with an array of known inputs and their corresponding outputs. Over time, the model 'learns' the relationship between these variables, using this knowledge to predict the outputs of fresh, unseen inputs.

Different models may be employed depending on the nature of the data and the prediction required. For instance, regression analysis can predict a continuous outcome like stock prices, while classification algorithms can predict which category a data point belongs to.

11.3. Big Data's Role in Accurate Forecasting

For an AI model to make accurate predictions, it requires large and diverse data sets. The more data the AI has to learn from, the better it understands the patterns and the more accurate its predictions are likely to be. This is where Big Data comes into play.

The advent of Big Data has drastically expanded the number of data points that can be processed. Traditional data sources such as financial records, customer databases, and experimental results are now bolstered with an explosion of data from web logs, social networks, sensor networks, and more, providing a much more detailed and representative set of data for machine learning algorithms to learn from.

The sheer volume, velocity, and variety of Big Data might be its most apparent features, but the real value lies in its granularity and the potential to capture complexity that traditional sources cannot.

11.4. Practical Applications of AI in Forecasting

AI-powered predictive modeling is becoming an integral part of numerous sectors. Businesses are using AI to forecast sales, manage supply chains, and prevent costly downtimes by predicting equipment failures. Governments are leveraging AI to predict traffic conditions, assess public health risks, and optimize energy consumption. A few examples include:

- **Sales forecasting**: Businesses use machine learning algorithms to analyze historical sales data and market conditions, predicting future sales and informing decisions about inventory management, budgeting, and strategic planning.

- **Traffic management**: Transportation departments are implementing AI models to predict traffic patterns based on historical data and real-time inputs from a network of sensors and cameras. The result is more efficient traffic flow and better resource allocation.

- **Public health**: AI is used to predict disease outbreaks or progression based on healthcare records, genetic data, and environmental factors, helping in faster response and mitigation.

11.5. Navigating Challenges in AI and Forecasting

As promising as AI and Big Data are in the realm of forecasting, they are not devoid of challenges. Algorithms can only learn from the data they've been trained on, and thus predictions can be biased or incomplete if the input data is. Strategies such as using diverse data sets and implementing bias-correction methods can address this.

Another common challenge is 'overfitting', where an AI model captures too much noise along with the signal from a training dataset and fails to generalize well to new datasets. Techniques such as cross-validation and regularization can help check overfitting.

Furthermore, the proper application of AI and Big Data forecasting requires a deep understanding of the methodologies and their limitations, emphasizing the need for adequate training, holistic strategy, and ethical considerations in AI deployment.

In sum, AI and Big Data hold the power to transform the way we predict and prepare for the future. By understanding and addressing their inherent complexities and potentials, we can tread towards a future where decisions are made not merely on intuition, but on data-driven insight, ensuring more reliable outcomes and transforming the world we live in.

Chapter 12. From Raw Data to Strategic Decisions: Insight Generation

Without a doubt, the foundational step in any data-driven approach is the collection, curation, and understanding of raw data. It is from this raw information that organizations harvest meaningful insights that power strategic decisions.

12.1. The Importance of Raw Data in Decision Making

Raw data refers to data collected from various sources, that has not undergone thorough processing, cleaning, or analysis. This information is often untidy, unstructured, and includes a significant amount of irrelevant and redundant data. Despite its disorganized nature, raw data embodies the purest form of truth about an organization, its processes, and its environment. On this basis, raw data remains an indispensable resource in decision-making processes across levels and alignments of strategic planning.

When correctly harnessed, raw data feeds the decision-making process by providing a factual foundation for predictions and analyses. For instance, financial institutions frequently use raw data to quantify risk and decide on acceptable levels of exposure, while healthcare institutions rely on it to detect diseases and optimize patient care strategies.

12.2. Data Collection and Curation

Data collection refers to the systematic gathering of data from a variety of sources, such as sensors, social media platforms, business transactions, and public data repositories. Care must be taken to ensure data's accuracy, totality, and relevance to the target analysis or decision-making process.

Once data collection is complete, data curation becomes crucial. This involves organizing, integrating, and enhancing collected data to ensure it is accurate, reliable, and usable. The data curation process includes data cleaning, annotation, integration, and archiving, all designed to improve the quality of raw data and make it ready for analysis.

12.3. From Raw Data to Processed Data

Processing raw data involves a series of transformations designed to convert it into a more interpretable and usable format. This step often requires advanced algorithms and computational procedures. Transformation activities include sorting, classifying, and coding the data. Other tasks could involve the elimination of outliers or removal of incomplete or erroneous data entries. Once adequately processed, the data is then ready for analysis.

12.4. Understanding and Leveraging Big Data

The sheer volume, variety, and velocity of big data present unique challenges to organizations. However, these challenges are offset by big data's potential for insight generation.

At its core, big data analysis revolves around the discovery of hidden patterns, correlations, and trends. Predictive analyses and machine learning algorithms can be used to unearth insights from this data, further abetting decision-making processes. For example, in eCommerce, big data can help understand customer behavior patterns and preferences, enabling businesses to personalize their service offerings and enrich the customer experience accordingly.

12.5. Insight Generation: The Final Step

Insight generation is the crowning stage of data analysis. Comprehensive in scope, it entails the transformation of refined data into actionable intelligence. The information yielded here is often used to guide strategic decisions, enabling organizations to innovate, compete, and excel.

Artificial Intelligence (AI) increasingly plays a crucial role in this phase. Machine learning models fed with processed data can predict outcomes, inform decisions, and trigger strategic actions. Advanced visualization tools are also used to communicate these insights effectively to decision makers.

We live in an era inundated by data. Turning this raw information into strategic decisions can often seem like a daunting task. However, achieving this transformative process requires understanding the value of raw data, embracing meticulous data collection and curation practices, intelligently processing and analyzing this data, and using AI tools to generate and communicate deep insights. Companies that master these processes possess an invaluable edge in today's digital, data-driven world. Their ability to make informed decisions based on actionable intelligence sets them apart, aiding in continuous growth and advancement.

Chapter 13. Current Applications: Who's Using AI and Big Data

Artificial Intelligence (AI) and Big Data have decisively entered many areas of human activity. They improve decision-making processes, facilitate operations, and offer new capabilities, all while managing multifaceted quantities of data that was previously unreachable. Together, they form an innovative and compelling way of transforming raw data into potent insights.

13.1. Healthcare

Within the healthcare sector, AI and Big Data are being used to revolutionize patient care, diagnostics, and research. Machine Learning (ML), a subset of AI, is particularly prominent here, with algorithms trained to recognize patterns in large datasets, facilitating early detection of diseases. For instance, scientists use Big Data analytics to spot trends in population health, aiding in infectious disease control. In clinical contexts, ML algorithms aid in streamlining diagnosis, particularly in fields like radiology or pathology where image recognition can be automated.

Pharmaceutical companies are leveraging AI to accelerate drug discovery, particularly in identifying viable candidates for further testing. For instance, AI company Atomwise uses its technology to predict which molecules might effectively block a certain protein related to a disease, which accelerates the preclinical drug discovery process.

13.2. Retail and E-Commerce

E-commerce has been a fertile sector for the application of AI and Big Data. Companies like Amazon and Alibaba exploit user browsing and purchasing data to predict customer behaviors, interests, and future purchases. They deploy recommendation systems, which operate on ML algorithms capable of noting correlations or copurchases among hundreds of millions of products.

AI tools also optimize supply chain and logistics. Forecasting equipment failures or prioritizing maintenance tasks in the distribution network are example applications. Delivery networks such as Amazon Prime Air, for instance, are beginning to rely on AI for facilitating sorting processes, predicting package volumes, and optimizing routes.

13.3. Finance and Insurance

Financial institutions utilize AI and Big Data to augment risk assessment, fraud detection, and investment strategies. AI is employed to detect anomalous trading patterns or suspicious transactions in real-time, much quicker than traditional methods.

Insurance companies, too, are adopting AI and Big Data. They are used to predict accurately insurance risks, automate claims processing, and even anticipate fraudulent claims. For example, auto insurers use telematics - a method of monitoring a vehicle, collecting data like speed and distance traveled, to adjust insurance premiums accordingly.

13.4. Agriculture

The fusion of AI and Big Data is revolutionizing farming as well. This approach, called precision agriculture, uses AI-powered drones and sensors to gather data on weather conditions, soil quality, crop maturity, and even pest presence. Machine learning algorithms analyze this data and provide farmers with precise real-time information, thus enabling them to make better decisions about when to plant, fertilize, or irrigate their fields.

13.5. Smart Cities

AI and Big Data are key enabling technologies for smart cities. They are used in traffic management where AI can analyze data collected from GPS and traffic sensors, providing actionable information to streamline traffic, reduce congestion, optimise public transportation routes, or for the planning and design of infrastructure.

13.6. Manufacturing

In manufacturing, AI and Big Data are used to increase efficiency, facilitate predictive maintenance, and improve product quality. They form the backbone of the fourth industrial revolution, enabling the rise of smart factories, where machines 'communicate' and cooperate with each other and with humans in real-time.

In conclusion, while AI and Big Data are still maturing technologies, their potential benefits are vast. The various cases described above represent a snapshot of the ongoing applications and innovations, demonstrating how these technologies are transforming our world and laying the groundwork for the future - a future where AI and Big Data will certainly continue reshaping industries in ways we can barely anticipate. This is not an exhaustive overview and a reader is advised to delve deeper into each industry to fully understand the extent of these applications.

Chapter 14. Navigating Potential Pitfalls and Ethical Considerations

Artificial Intelligence (AI) and Big Data have together evolved into a pertinent force, unlocking unprecedented capabilities and opportunities across sectors. However, in parallel to their potential, these twin technologies also bring about a set of challenges and ethical qualms that need careful understanding and navigation. This vivid exploration is an examination designed to educate on these potential pitfalls and provide a framework to address ethical considerations when implementing and exploiting AI and Big Data initiatives.

===Understanding the Potential Pitfalls

The progression of AI and Big Data, as well as their increased adoption, has led to the rise of potential pitfalls that participants need to be wary of. These pitfalls range from technical difficulties and strategic errors to issues arising out of non-compliance with data privacy rules.

1. **Data Quality and Consistency**: AI systems perform only as well as the data they consume. Poor data quality, including biases, inconsistencies, and errors in the collected data can greatly affect the accuracy of AI analyses and predictions. Therefore, organizations need to ensure the integrity and quality of data to avoid misleading outputs.

2. **Security Concerns**: Exploiting Big Data involves harnessing vast amounts of organizational and personal information, making the entire ecosystem a prime target for cyber-attacks. Stringent security systems and practices need to be in place to prevent data leaks and safeguard sensitive information.

3. **Integration Challenges**: The integration of AI and Big Data with existing systems and processes sometimes proves to be a challenging task. There might be compatibility issues, and the staff might also need extensive training to comfortably work with the new systems.

4. **High Costs**: AI and Big Data initiatives often involve significant investment in technology, infrastructure, and skilled personnel. These costs can be a significant hurdle, especially for small businesses and startups.

5. **Compliance Risks**: With stringent laws regarding data privacy and usage being enacted worldwide, there is a high risk of non-compliance due to the complexity and extensive coverage of these laws. Noncompliance can lead to severe penalties and reputational damage.

===Addressing Ethical Concerns

In tandem with the pitfalls is the reign of ethical considerations. If overlooked, these could spell significant social, legal, and reputational risks for organizations utilizing AI and Big Data.

1. **Privacy**: The aggregation and analysis of data often intrude on people's privacy. Intricately understanding the fine line between utilization and invasion is critical, and consent from data subjects should be integral to practices.

2. **Data Bias**: Datasets may contain inherent biases, which if not identified and corrected, could lead to discriminatory or unfair practices propagated further by AI systems.

3. **Transparency**: The decision-making processes within AI systems is often "black box", leading to a lack of transparency. Users have the right to know how their data is being processed and how decisions that affect them are being made.

4. **Accountability**: The question of who holds responsibility for decisions made by AI systems is increasingly pressing. Clear lines

of accountability, therefore, need to be defined.

===Strategic Measures for Mitigating Risks

Understanding the potential downfalls and ethical considerations is just half the battle. The real challenge lies in incorporating strategic measures to mitigate these risks.

1. **Invest in Data Governance**: Organizations should have cross-functional data governance teams to ensure data quality, data security, data privacy, and regulatory compliance are met comprehensively.

2. **Implement Robust Security Measures**: Fortify security infrastructure with advanced technologies such as data encryption, usage of firewalls, intrusion detection systems and conduct regular security audits to identify potential weaknesses.

3. **Train and Educate Personnel**: Provide regular training sessions about the importance of Data Accuracy, Data Security, Data Ethics, and Regulatory Compliance.

4. **Establish Fair and Transparent Data Practices**: A high degree of transparency can be maintained by providing ample information about data collection, processing, storage, and utilization protocols.

5. **Develop Ethical AI systems**: Invest in developing "Explainable AI" to enhance transparency and eliminate biases from datasets. Understanding of the ethical implications should guide the creation and execution of AI models.

14.1. In Conclusion: Balancing Potential with Prudence

The confluence of AI and Big Data indeed presents substantial opportunities. However, to fully harness their potential while sidestepping pitfalls, organizations must approach with prudence. Awareness of possible pitfalls with active measures put in place to counter them, and reverence for ethical considerations should form the foundation for all AI and Big Data implementations. By embedding these strategies into practices, organizations can open themselves up to amazing possibilities, all while maintaining trust and upholding their ethical principles.

Chapter 15. Looking Ahead: The Disruptive Potential of AI and Big Data

As we embark on our journey into the future, we are met with buzzwords that have become the anthem of this data-driven era - AI and Big Data. These leviathans promise to disrupt the very way we live, work, and think, forging a new era of innovation, productivity, and digital intelligence.

15.1. The Future is Data-driven

The future, as experts predict, will be data-driven. As technology starts to integrate more meaningfully into our lives, every action, decision, and interaction will register as a data point, feeding into sprawling databases stored in the cloud. From multinational corporations to individual users, data will be the currency of the future, driving both economies and societies.

Big Data, characterized by its volume, variety, and velocity, is the backbone of this data-driven future. Tapping into and understanding this huge pool of information calls for advanced analysis techniques - where AI steps in.

Artificial Intelligence, in its many forms, will be able to decode the disparate and unstructured data points to create comprehensible patterns that can guide decision-making processes. With innovations such as machine learning and data mining, AI algorithms can delve into the massive volumes of data and bring forth insightful narratives hidden within its depths.

15.2. AI: Redefining Industries and Lives

No industry is immune to the transformative potential AI wields. From healthcare to financial services, from logistics to media, AI is all set to revamp how sectors operate.

In healthcare, for instance, AI platforms can analyze vast amounts of patient data to predict disease patterns, allocate resources, and personalize treatment plans. AI could significantly reduce medical errors, enable early disease detection, and optimize healthcare supply chains. According to Accenture, AI applications can create up to $150 billion in annual savings for the U.S. healthcare economy by 2026.

On the other end of the spectrum, in industries like financial services, AI and Big Data can catalyze a higher level of sophistication in operations and customer interactions. Complex algorithms are already making stock predictions, managing portfolios, and detecting fraudulent activity with remarkable accuracy. Opportunities for automation will revolutionize banking, insurance, and asset management.

Beyond industries, AI will redefine lives. Smart home technology, advanced personal assistants, autonomous cars, personalized recommendations – the personal applications of AI are vast and continually expanding.

15.3. Our Interaction With Technology: A Paradigm Shift

In many tangible weays, AI will reform how we interact with technology. User interfaces will shift from tactile (keyboards and touch screens) to experiential, ranging from voice-enabled AI systems to immersive AR and VR experiences. An AI-powered tech environment means molding technology to fit our lives, as opposed to us adapting to technological challenges.

AI will recognize our voices, understand our habits, anticipate our needs, and act upon this knowledge. It will embed itself in our day-to-day lives, invisible yet impactful. This shift will also redefine the essence of accessibility, opening doors for those previously challenged by traditional interaction models.

15.4. Ethical Dilemmas: The Road Ahead

While we can marvel at the potential of AI and Big Data, we must also address the emerging ethical dilemmas. As AI algorithms make more decisions, issues of fairness, accountability, and transparency come to the fore.

A prominent concern is data privacy and handling. With the creation and use of massive data sets, ensuring the integrity and confidentiality of individual data is vital. Regulations like the EU's General Data Protection Regulation (GDPR) are attempts to ensure that the right frameworks are in place.

Another ethical aspect to consider is algorithmic fairness. As AI applications make life-altering decisions, it's crucial to ensure that these algorithms are fair, unbiased, and transparent. Scrutiny of AI's decision-making process is a field that requires concerted efforts from researchers, policymakers, and organizations alike.

15.5. Building a Sustainable AI Future

To ensure a sustainable AI-infused future, policies and frameworks guiding AI use need to be robust. Regulatory policies should be designed to navigate between innovation and public safety. They should provide an environment conducive to AI and Big Data's growth, while also protecting society and individuals from possible misuse.

Organizations investing in AI should focus on building AI systems that are explainable, transparent, and fair. Empowering people by building digital literacy will be essential. If handled responsibly, the disruptive potential of AI and Big Data promises to pave the way for a future that is more productive, efficient, and fundamentally smarter.

In conclusion, AI and Big Data are not just components of the digital transformation narrative. They are indeed the narrative itself. The future we envisage relies heavily on how effectively and ethically we leverage these technologies. It's an exciting yet challenging road ahead. However, armed with the right knowledge, tools, and ethics, we can harness the true potential of AI and Big Data, driving us towards an era of unimagined possibilities.